✦ Front cover : the 102nd R.I. from Paris and Chartres attached to the 7th D.I. fought in Belgium in August, where it suffered heavy losses. The regiment retreated and took part in the Battle of the Marne, in Nanteuil, where its soldiers famously travelled to the battlefields by taxi.

OREP
EDITIONS

OREP Éditions, Zone tertiaire de Nonant, 14400 BAYEUX
Tél.: 02 31 51 81 31 - **Fax:** 02 31 51 81 32
E-mail: info@orepeditions.com - **Web:** www.orepeditions.com
Éditor: Grégory PIQUE
Graphique design: Éditions OREP
Layout: Laurent SAND
Translated from the french by: Sam Brown

ISBN : 978-2-8151-0283-5 - **Copyright OREP 2016**
Legal Deposit: 1ˢᵗ quarter 2016

On les aura !

INTRODUCTION

Coëtquidan, le 9-7-14

FROM PEACE TO WAR

What this conscript did not know at the time he wrote this card was that his training would be put into effect twenty-four days later ... Indeed, when Archduke Franz-Ferdinand was assassinated on 28 June 1914 in Sarajevo, Europe entered a war that would last four years and cause more than 8.5 million victims.

*Souvenir d'un
ami en manœuvre
à Coëtquidan —
heureusement qu'elle se
termine demain
Bien le bonjour
à Jeanne à Gaspard
à Chavaloir
Chie*

FROM A WAR OF MOVEMENT TO A WAR OF POSITION :

✦ The 16th R.I. from Clermont-Ferrand, attached to the 25th D.I., was transferred by rail to eastern France in August before taking part in France's first victorious offensives in Epinal. In September, the Regiment was based in Xaffeviller in the Vosges.

The infantrymen mobilised on 2 August 1914 were equipped very similarly to their predecessors of 1870.

After a great amount of fighting in the Vosges and in Lorraine, which ended with the loss of forts, the French army obtained its first victory during the battle of the Marne from the 5th to the 10th of September. After four months of constant fighting, the army had been bled white. The race to the sea concluded with a German defeat, since they failed to break through allied lines. The French staff, which had hoped for a short, straightforward victory thanks to their troops' mobility, was forced to rethink its strategy. The war of movement had ended.

From November onwards, the front lines were stabilised. The troops dug in and took refuge in trenches. The war of movement gave way to a war of position. The "garance" uniform, with its bright red trousers, proved to be completely unsuited to wartime conditions as it was far too visble for the Germans, whose infantry had an entirely field-grey uniform.

As early as September, it was decided to change the uniform by simplifying it and switching to light blue, known as «bleu horizon» from 1915. However, the dreadful losses of the summer of 1914 had depleted uniform and equipment stocks.
As a consequence, some units had to keep the original blue and red uniform until 1915, trying their best to cover up their red trousers. Other units were given militarised civilian clothing (especially corduroy trousers and tunics/jackets) as well as old equipment, some of which dated back to the Second Empire period of 1850 – 1870.

The same applied for weapons because the summer's losses could not be immediately compensated. In the trenches, soldiers often improvised and created new weapons, such as grenade-throwing crossbows. Antique fifty-year old siege mortars were also reused.

The entire supply chain had been organised with a war of movement in mind, and certainly not for a front made up of more than 1,000 kilometers of trenches.

SEPTEMBER 1914 : THE MARNE

✦ Worn on the back, the pack consisted of a Mle 1893 haversack - also known as Azor in military slang - with its cover, and a Mle 1852 mess tin. The third ammunition pouch was visible as well as the Mle 1881 canvas water bucket attached to the haversack. The Mle 1892 satchel contained spare boots, supplies, cutlery and personal effects.

✦ An infantryman of the 58th R.I. from Avignon and the Vaucluse region, which took part in the Battle of the Marne in September 1914. This soldier is wearing a Mle 1884 kepi with its Mle 1913 cover, a Mle 1877 iron-blue greatcoat, a Mle 1845 belt and buckle, Mle 1892 braces, Mle 1888 ammunition pouches, a Mle 1892 satchel, a one-litre Mle 1877 flask with its Mle 1867 drinking cup, Mle 1867 trousers with Mle 1912 boots and Mle 1913 puttees. He is armed with a Mle 1886/93 Lebel rifle with its Mle 1888 hook-quillon bayonet.

✦ The 36th R.I., stationed in the Caen castle, was sent to Belgium in August. It then retreated before taking part in the Battle of the Marne in September, south of Reims. At the end of the year the Regiment was in the Aisne region.

✦ The 329th R.I. was the reserve regiment of the 129th R.I. from Le Havre. It was sent to Charleroi before retreating and being sent to the Battle of the Marne where it fought near Montmirail.

* Mle : pattern
* R. I : Infantry regiment

INDIVIDUAL AND COLLECTIVE WEAPONS

As well as weapons, the soldiers had to carry what they needed for life in the field. For food, they were equipped with a mess tin, cutlery and a 1.5 litre water bottle. They also carried a Mle 1887 tent half for shelter.

It was common for soldiers to have other personal items in addition to the regulation pack, such as letters, objects bought back home, found in ruined houses or taken from the enemy.

✦ Smoking was a way to kill time and to warm up in the cold winter months. This lighter is made from an ammunition cartridge, the tobacco is kept in a modified German ammunition pouch.

✦ A Mle 1852 mess tin and a Mle 1852 drinking cup carried on the water bottle.

✦ The Mle 1881 indentity tag, worn on the wrist, was essential for identification. The personal booklet was carried in the greatcoat and was used as an identification document. The booklet and tag pictured here belonged to a soldier named Vuillemin, visible on the left-hand side of the photograph.

✦ A Mle 1910 Montjardet lantern with its case containing two candles and a civilian candle holder.

✦ Sewing and cleaning equipment.

✦ The cutlery, a biscuit tin and a box of chocolates are displayed here on a patriotic handkerchief celebrating the Allies.

PORTABLE TOOLS – INDIVIDUAL AND COLLECTIVE

✦ A pickaxe and its cover.

✦ An axe and its cover.

✦ A Seurre Mle 1909 intrenching tool.

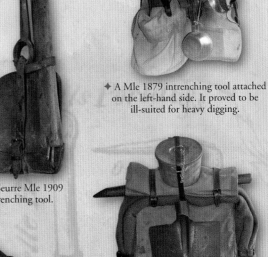

✦ A Mle 1879 intrenching tool attached on the left-hand side. It proved to be ill-suited for heavy digging.

✦ Foldable Mle 1879 saw and its ammunition pouch shaped pouch.

✦ A haversack holding the metal head of the Mle 1916 round shovel.

✦ A billhook and its leather cover.

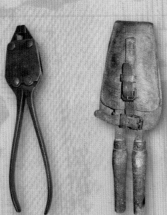

✦ Mle 1905 wire-cutters and cover, an essential tool for cutting barbed wire.

✦ The billhook was attached to the haversack with the collective cooking dixie (Mle 1887). Four of these dixies were issued per platoon.

THE OFFICER ON CAMPAIGN

WARRANT OFFICER "ADJUDANT"
OF THE 163RD R.I. FROM NICE

Pictured here is in fact a uniform of a non-commissioned officer which is identical to that worn by warrant officers. Most officers were Saint-Cyr graduates where they underwent a two-year period of training. On the 2nd of August, the Montmirail class was mobilised despite not having completed its training and sent directly to garrisons or to the front lines. Among these young officers was de Lattre de Tassigny, as well as my grandfather, who was sent to Manonviller, where he was taken prisoner 26 days later. Only 288 men out of the 456 of the Montmirail promotion lived to see 1919.

✦ A Mle 1882 issue sabre. It was worn for show at the very beginning of the war, but was subsequently abandoned as it was a somewhat cumbersome and useless weapon.

✦ A Mle 1892 revolver and its holster. Pictured here is the one that belonged to my grandfather, which he kept during his time as a prisoner of war. It is dated 1914.

✦ Binoculars became a regulation item of campaign equipment on 6 June 1890. It is worth noting the dimensions of an infantryman and a cavalryman on the copper plates.

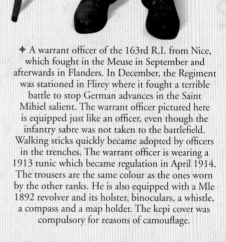

✦ The 202nd R.I. from Granville on a war footing in August 1914. The Staff Lieutenant-colonel is in the foreground. In August, the regiment fought in the Ardennes attached to the 60th D.I. before retreating and fighting in the Meuse. It took part in the Battle of the Marne in September. In December, the Regiment was in the Champagne region where it fought in terrible battles, particurlarly at the Moulin de Souain.

✦ A warrant officer of the 163rd R.I. from Nice, which fought in the Meuse in September and afterwards in Flanders. In December, the Regiment was stationed in Flirey where it fought a terrible battle to stop German advances in the Saint Mihiel salient. The warrant officer pictured here is equipped just like an officer, even though the infantry sabre was not taken to the battlefield. Walking sticks quickly became adopted by officers in the trenches. The warrant officer is wearing a 1913 tunic which became regulation in April 1914. The trousers are the same colour as the ones worn by the other ranks. He is also equipped with a Mle 1892 revolver and its holster, binoculars, a whistle, a compass and a map holder. The kepi cover was compulsory for reasons of camouflage.

TRENCH WARFARE AND THE GREAT OFFENSIVES

In the winter of 1914, the French infantry lived in trenches that the autumn rain had turned into mudbaths.

The cold and snow literally froze operations. The supply corps had not made provisions for equipment suited to such weather, forcing the soldiers to wear animal skins, jumpers, scarves and various other pieces of clothing sent to them by relatives or found in destroyed and abandoned villages. The war, which was supposed to have been short, had turned into siege warfare, with each side living a precarious existence in trenches, despite the fact that the high command had planned nothing to cope with such conditions. In order to recognize the survivors of 1914, the Croix de Guerre medal was created on 4 February 1915; two million soldiers were awarded the medal during the war.

April the 22nd is a date to remember as it saw the first ever use of toxic gas (chlorine) in Ypres (Belgium). The soldiers panicked since they had no means to protect themselves against this new type of weapon which killed 3,000 men on this day.

By the end of the war, 1.2 million men had been gassed, 91,000 of whom were killed. Gas and other new weapons such as aviation and flamethrowers were developed in the early phases of the war and contributed to the war's rising death toll.

The spring saw the launching of large-scale offensives from the Vosges to the North of France in order to break through enemy lines and restart a war of movement and thus defeat the enemy faster. It was in this context that Joffre famously said "Je les grignote" – which translates literally as "I am nibbling them», an expression which sums up well 1915.

Les Eparges, Notre-Dame-de-Lorette, le Vieil-Armand :
All these names have become symbols of this "nibbling", for which thousands of soldiers died in order to gain (or lose...) a few metres of ground.
Germany, which was better prepared, had many machine-guns as well as a strong artillery, killing and wounding many French soldiers.

In order to compensate for these losses, new drafts were mobilised and the army drew on all possible means to equip them. Stocks of equipment were depleted; consequently, equipment made of canvas and militarised civilian clothing were worn by the French infantryman.

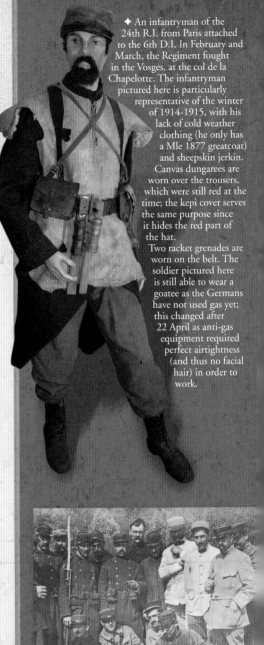

✦ An infantryman of the 24th R.I. from Paris attached to the 6th D.I. In February and March, the Regiment fought in the Vosges, at the col de la Chapelotte. The infantryman pictured here is particularly representative of the winter of 1914-1915, with his lack of cold weather clothing (he only has a Mle 1877 greatcoat) and sheepskin jerkin. Canvas dungarees are worn over the trousers, which were still red at the time; the kepi cover serves the same purpose since it hides the red part of the hat.
Two racket grenades are worn on the belt. The soldier pictured here is still able to wear a goatee as the Germans have not used gas yet; this changed after 22 April as anti-gas equipment required perfect airtightness (and thus no facial hair) in order to work.

✦ This picture of a group examining a Minenwerfer projectile is representative of the uniforms of 1915. The leather ammunition pouches have given way to canvas ones. Corduroy clothing was worn along with the Mle 1877 and Poiret Mle 1915 greatcoats. A spectacular-looking Gras rifle bayonet is also visible, even though it was no longer used in combat. The horizon blue colour is perfectly visible in this photograph.

THE METAMORPHOSIS

GAS

The first items for protection against gas were cotton pads soaked in hyposulfite and sodium carbonate, and airtight goggles. Many different models were created, but the C1 compresses and the P1 and P2 cotton pads were the most widespread.

✦ Tampon T compresses with anti-gas goggles (used from December 1915 onwards).

✦ The C1 compress was used from May 1915 onwards.

✦ The canvas holder for the C1 compress.

ERSATZ EQUIPMENT

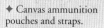

✦ Belt buckles were also painted blue.

✦ As cloth was rationned, wornout greatcoats were cut up and used as covers for Mle 1877 water bottles.

✦ The 18th R.I. from Pau saw action at the Battle of the Marne in 1914 with the 36th D.I. In 1915, the Regiment was based at Hurtebise farm on the Chemin des Dames in the Champagne region until the spring of 1916. The soldier's uniform here is entirely horizon blue. He is wearing a Poiret greatcoat with one row of buttons. The leather pieces of equipment were replaced with canvas as a stop gap measure due to shortages. The C1 holder containing anti-gas equipment was worn on the chest within easy reach, as were the goggle worn on the kepi. The trousers are a canvas stop-gap measure pattern.

✦ Canvas ammunition pouches and straps.

HEADWEAR

KEPIS

The use of artillery on a large scale was the cause of many headwounds because the cloth kepi provided no protection whatsoever. The supply services first provided the troops with a protective steel "cervelière" in March 1915, but this too proved to be somewhat useless.

✦ Mle 1914 kepi made in grey/blue cloth, with anti-gas goggles.

✦ This is a private-purchase kepi; its colour is more metallic than the regulation pattern headwear.

✦ Mle 1884 kepi with its Mle 1913 cover that leaves the regiment number visible.

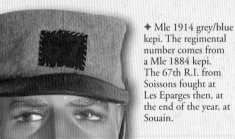

✦ Mle 1914 grey/blue kepi. The regimental number comes from a Mle 1884 kepi. The 67th R.I. from Soissons fought at Les Eparges then, at the end of the year, at Souain.

✦ A felt kepi with a peak made of the same material. The 409th R.I. from Châtellerault fought in the Somme in 1915.

THE 1915 ADRIAN HELMET

The Adrian helmet, named after its designer, was adopted on 10 May. In late August, it was issued on a wide scale to the troops on the front lines.

It was originally light blue, but was repainted in a darker blue from 1916 onwards. It was less efficient than its German counterpart, but nevertheless became a symbol of the Poilus. In late 1918, each soldier could bring home his helmet adorned with a plaque reading «A soldier of the Great War 1914-1918». In total, 20 million helmets were produced over three years. The outline of the infantryman was standardised with the introduction of the blue horizon uniform; only the branch of service insignia on the helmet helped to distinguish the various soldiers.

The photograph below depicts the issuing of helmets at the front line. The men are carrying their kepi while the helmets are still new and in their factory wrapping.

✦ Infantry. The same helmet was used by the Foreign Legion but in a mustard colour.

✦ Colonial infantry.

✦ Artillery.

✦ Light Infantry.

✦ Engineers.

✦ Medical services.

✦ African troops (Zouaves, Tirailleurs etc), with the typical mustard colour, identical to that of the Foreign Legion.

THE NEW OFFICERS' UNIFORM

In the same way as those of the other ranks, the officers' uniforms also underwent standardisation with the introduction of the horizon blue uniforms. The objective was of course to make them less visible to the enemy by blending in with the rest of the troops; this is why sabres, among other things, were removed from the front lines.

In 1915 there were many officers using private-purchase equipment to protect themselves from the cold and rain.

Behind the lines, an entire industry had developed in order to supply the soldiers with military-style clothing to be worn in addition to regulation equipment.

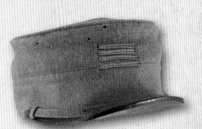

✦ Non-regulation kepi with a major's rank insignia.

✦ A divisional general's helmet (3 stars) with a platted chinstrap.

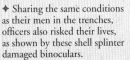

✦ Communication with the artillery was carried out with flares. Indeed, according to the colour of the flare, the artillery could adjust their fire. Since radio communication did not exist, flares were the only means to communicate with units behind the lines.

✦ Sharing the same conditions as their men in the trenches, officers also risked their lives, as shown by these shell splinter damaged binoculars.

✦ A lieutenant in a matching uniform. The sabre is only present for the photograph : it had long been abandoned for combat. The private-purchase kepi does not bear rank insignia. The rank bars (two for a lieutenant) are visible on the cuff of the right sleeve. The puttees are private-purchase, just like the boots. In combat, this lieutenant would be carrying a Mle 1893 revolver, a map holder and anti-gas equipment.

VERDUN: A TRAGEDY OF TWO NATIONS

1916 saw two of the Great War's most violent battles.

On February 21st, the German offensive at Verdun, as well as the capture of Fort Douaumont, served as a prelude to fierce French resistance.

Reinforcements and supplies were brought up day and night along the Voie Sacrée - the "Sacred Way" - between Verdun and Bar-le-Duc in order to make up for the huge losses. Soldiers were literally pulverised and crushed by artillery fire, machine-guns and of course gas attacks.

One million German shells were fired on the first day of the battle.

For the Poilus, moving up to the frontlines was often a one-way journey. It is estimated that each French regiment went through Verdun at least once, which gives us an idea of the scale of the human losses caused by the battle. Indeed, the rotaion of units allowed the men some respite and to bring in new drafts, which was not the case for the German army, in which the same regiments were used from beginning to end. For both France and Germany, Verdun has become synonymous with hell. The battle erased entire villages from the map forever.

Moreover, on July 1st saw the start of the Franco-British offensive in the Somme, resulting in a record 1.3 million losses (killed, wounded, or missing).

The year of 1916 and Verdun, due to the intensity of the fighting, have come to symbolize the Great War.

The familiar outline of the Poilu with his horizon blue uniform and Adrian helmet had now become an iconic image of the war.

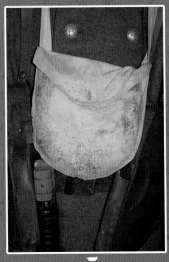

THEY SHALL NOT PASS - 44TH R.I. SOLDIER

Pictured here is a soldier of the 44th R.I. from Lons-le-Saulnier and Montbéliard. The Regiment was part of the 14th D.I. and fought in Verdun in early 1916, notably at Bezonvaux and the lake at Vaux. In August, the Regiment took part in the Battle of the Somme alongside the British. Finally, in October, they saw action in the Champagne region. The soldier here is wearing an almost definitive version of the uniform, that is to say a greatcoat with a double row of buttons and an Adrian helmet painted in a darker blue. The rifle is still a Lebel Mle 1886/93. The M2 gasmask is worn on the chest for quick access; its pouch is worn under the left ammunition pouch. The mask's transport satchel is also deployed. The soldier here has all his combat gear.

PERSONAL WEAPONS

✦ The racket grenade was just a piece of wood on which an explosive charge (melinite 100 g) had been attached with wire. Despite being dangerous to use, it was very popular at the beginning of the war.

GRENADES

Trench warfare meant that that the combatants existed in close proximity to one another. Small arms became impractical and the grenade emerged as an excellent weapon as it could be used in an offensive role whilst leaving the thrower under cover.

✦ A 400g grenade designed to destroy barbed wire. It was introduced in 1915.

Once again, France was behind Germany which already had many different types of grenades, such as fragmentation grenades.
First of all, old stocks, then makeshift grenades, such as tennis balls filled with gun powder, were used. 1915 saw the creation of the F1 grenade, which resembled what is now seen as the archetypal grenade with its fragmentation design for a wider dispersal of splinters.

During attacks, grenades were carried in the greatcoat pockets or in Mle 1861 satchels.

A grenade discharger was designed to fit on the end of the rifle in order to fire VB grenades.

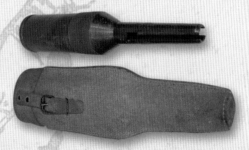

✦ The VB (Vivien-Bessières) grenade discharger was designed to be fixed to the end of any rifle. It allowed grenades to be fired further and with more accuracy as the rifle could be wedged into a set position. A soldier could throw a grenade 35 metres on average; a VB, on the other hand, could be fired to a range of approximately 190 metres.

✦ An explosive VB grenade next to a parachute flare which could also be fired from the launcher in order to illuminate No Man's Land.

a. P1 Mle 1915 grenade.
b. Besozzi Grenade, first imported from Italy in 1915, then made in France.
c1. Citron Foug grenade, introduced in 1916.
c2. Citron Foug grenade in its original sheet metal protection.
d. Mle 1847 grenade with a Mle 1882 fuze.
e. F1 grenade (Mle 1915) with an impact igniter.
f. Same model, with a BA Mle 1916.

REVOLVERS AND PISTOLS

When it came to handguns, the army had two main regulation revolvers : the 1873 issued for use in rear-echelon areas and its replacement, the 8mm calibre 1892 pattern. They were used by officers and non-commissioned officers, but also by certain specialist soldiers, such as machine-gun crews for close-quarter defence.

Due to low stocks and many guns being lost, the French army had to order many revolvers from Spain, which were copies of American weapons such as Smith & Wesson models and Colts. The most famous was the 7.65mm Ruby, which was manufactured in Eibar.

✦ For economic and practical reasons in terms of manufacturing, the holster for the Mle 1892 revolver was simplified.

✦ The 7.65 mm Ruby automatic pistol and its holster was manufactured by many Spanish companies. The Ruby was one of the many weapons that were ordered in large quantities from Spain.

✦ A Chauchat machine-gunner equipped with a Ruby pistol.

✦ A pack of 8mm bullets.

✦ A French and German handgun side by side : the Mle 1892 and the P08. The P08 proved to be more sensitive to muddy conditions whereas the Mle 1892 was of a more basic design.

RIFLES

It was in 1886, when a new type of smokeless gunpowder was invented, that a new rifle, the Lebel, was introduced; it was meant to replace the standard issue Gras rifles that were in use at the time. It was modified in 1893 and received its definitive name : the Lebel 1886 M 93. Its faults became obvious during the war, such as its length and its tendency to become fouled up. Since a great amount of Lebel rifles were in stock, the rifle was used until the end of the war, even though new troops received Berthier 07-15 rifles.

The Berthier proved to be more practical with its loading mechanism able to take three-round chargers, increased to five in 1916 (07-15M16).

1917 also saw the introduction of the semi-automatic Mle 17 rifle which was reserved for soldiers with good shooting skills due to its complexity. However, this weapon did not see widespread issue.

Other units such as artillery or cavalry, were equipped with shorter carbines as rifles were too cumbersome.

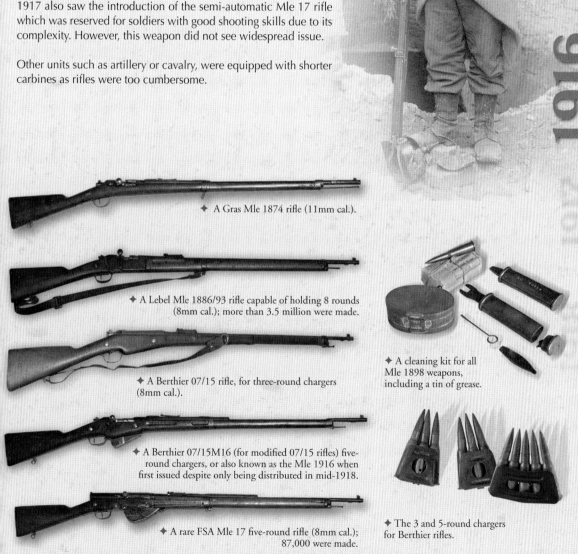

✦ A Gras Mle 1874 rifle (11mm cal.).

✦ A Lebel Mle 1886/93 rifle capable of holding 8 rounds (8mm cal.); more than 3.5 million were made.

✦ A Berthier 07/15 rifle, for three-round chargers (8mm cal.).

✦ A cleaning kit for all Mle 1898 weapons, including a tin of grease.

✦ A Berthier 07/15M16 (for modified 07/15 rifles) five-round chargers, or also known as the Mle 1916 when first issued despite only being distributed in mid-1918.

✦ A rare FSA Mle 17 five-round rifle (8mm cal.); 87,000 were made.

✦ The 3 and 5-round chargers for Berthier rifles.

BAYONETS AND DAGGERS

The 52cm long Lebel bayonet was nicknamed "Rosalie". Long and sharp, its quadrangular blade inflicted serious wounds, but its length was a disadvantage in the trenches since it made it difficult to use.

At the beginning of the war, the bayonet had a quillon (for stacking rifles in camp) which were impractical in the trenches as they often got caught in the barbed wire. It was deleted in late 1914. However, many broken bayonets were recut in order to make short daggers which were a lot easier to handle in a hand-to-hand fight.

As a consequence, in 1915, many soldiers were in possession of all sorts of daggers, the most famous of which being the «vengeur de 1870» - the avenger of 1870. Some soldiers even had butchers' knives ...

Once again, the army turned to old stocks and used all means at their disposal.

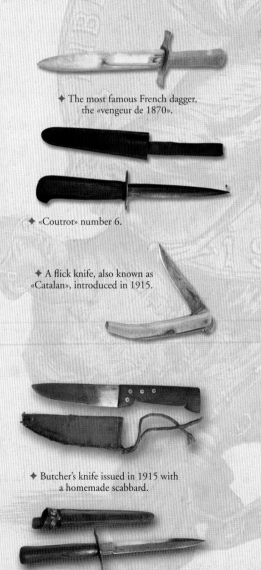

✦ The most famous French dagger, the «vengeur de 1870».

✦ «Coutrot» number 6.

✦ A flick knife, also known as «Catalan», introduced in 1915.

✦ Butcher's knife issued in 1915 with a homemade scabbard.

✦ A "vengeur de 1870" and its leather scabbard.

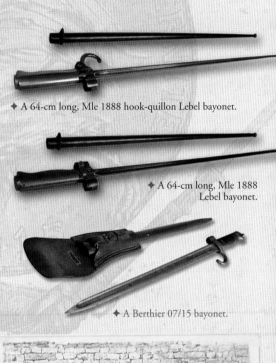

✦ A 64-cm long, Mle 1888 hook-quillon Lebel bayonet.

✦ A 64-cm long, Mle 1888 Lebel bayonet.

✦ A Berthier 07/15 bayonet.

✦ The soldier on the left is proudly displaying his butchers' knife.

THE SACRIFICE OF THE CHEMIN DES DAMES

The attack on the Chemin des Dames in the Champagne region and the mutinies, which were followed by executions, were the two major events of 1917.

After three years of fighting, the army was on its knees. The war, which had been expected to be short, proved to be longer than expected. Everyone had family members who had been killed or wounded in the war. France was still partly occupied and there had been huge destruction.

War on such a massive scale was unprecedented.

Germany, despite the allied blockade, did not give up and kept mobilising younger troops to make up for its losses.

It was in this context that the offensive on the Chemin des Dames prepared by General Nivelle was launched. Since the preliminary artillery bombing had been deliberately light in order to retain an element of surprise, the subsequent battle was a bloodbath, with the Germans safely sheltered in their trenches with their artillery and machine-guns.

Entire regiments were wiped out during the attack, and only small groups of soldiers were able to regain their trenches, leaving behind their dead and wounded in No-Man's Land. From day one, the attack was a failure, but Nivelle persevered nonetheless. As a consequence, approximately 40,000 men died during the battle.

There had been a few isolated cases of rebellion in the first three years of the war, but the Chemin des Dames proved too much for the demoralised and exhausted soldiers, outraged by the indifference of their superiors regarding human losses.

First of all, court martials were set up for desertion and the abandoning of positions, leading to executions which only exacerbated the soldiers' outrage.

It took the sacking of Nivelle and his replacement by General Pétain to appease the mutineers. Pétain started by decreasing the use of capital punishment, then attempted to improve the soldiers' lives and, most notably, reintroduced leave for the soldiers. The United States' entry in the war on April 6th came as a relief, but the American troops that arrived in Saint-Nazaire lacked combat experience. However, they made up for the collapse of Russia and its subsequent signing of a peace treaty with Germany on December 7th after suffering from revolutionary movements and numerous military defeats.

In terms of equipment, not much changed. The horizon blue uniform became standard and technological advances were in great part reserved for aviation which was now seen and used as a weapon in itself. The first use of tanks by the British at Flers in the Somme on 15 September stunned the Germans. French tanks first saw action at Berry-au-Bac but, due to a lack of infantry support, the attack was a failure.

Things were to be different in 1918 with the large-scale arrival of the Renault FT17 tanks accompanied by infantry support, something that played a vital role in the final victory.

✦ Following the mutinies, periods of leave were reinstated. The Chauchat gunner pictured here has made the most of his leave to have his picture taken with his wife after spending one year on the front line.
He is proudly wearing his Croix de Guerre. His regiment, the 42nd R.I. from Belfort, suffered great losses at the Chemin des Dames.

COLLECTIVE WEAPONS

MACHINE-GUNS

Despite not being a recent invention, machine-guns completely changed the way battles were fought. Their firepower rendered bayonet attacks and charges over open terrain obsolete.

But French tactics differed totally to those used by the Germans. Indeed, the Germans used machine-guns in groups, enabling them to use crossfire to halt any ground offensives. The huge death toll of the first weeks of the war bear witness to this.

In the French army, machine-guns were not used in groups and without a precise purpose, which is why they were less effective.

Later on, the experience of the first months of the war changed the way these weapons were used. Their average rate of fire of approximately 400/500 rounds per minute allowed three main types of use : harrassing fire consisting of sporadic shooting to damage enemy morale ; barrage fire to render a given area unreachable ; and finally neutralisation to prevent enemy troops from using their own weapons.

They also realised at last that machine-guns could support infantry troops, leading the French to adopt German tactical methods.

It took thousands of deaths in 1914 to reach these conclusions and the names on the war memorials are there to remind us of this...

There were two main types of machine-guns : the Hotchkiss Mle 1914 and the Saint Etienne Mle 1907 ; the latter's complexity would eventually make it unpopular, since it was less straightforward to use than the Hotchkiss.
Nevertheless, both were used in combat.

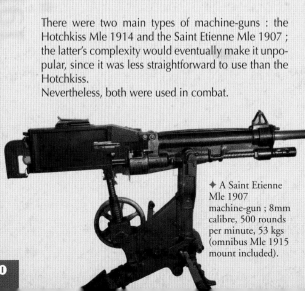

✦ A Saint Etienne Mle 1907 machine-gun ; 8mm calibre, 500 rounds per minute, 53 kgs (omnibus Mle 1915 mount included).

✦ A 25 round (8mm) strip.

✦ Maintenance kit for the Hotchkiss Mle 1914.

✦ Hotchkiss Mle 1914 machine gun.
500 rounds per minute, 8mm calibre, 52 kgs
(Mle 1916 mount included).

The box for the 250-round culated metal belt for Hotchkiss chine-guns.

✦ The complexity of the Saint Etienne machine-gun soon rendered it unpopular in comparison with the Hotchkiss.

✦ Mle 1915 boxes used to transport twelve 25-round strips.

FM CHAUCHAT GUNNER

CHEMIN DES DAMES, 1917

The Chauchat Mle 1915 was the first automatic rifle to be issued on a large scale, as early as 1915. Despite its many faults, such as its open semi-circular magazine that was prone to getting clogged with mud, the weapon brought significant firepower and provided support fire.

Indeed, as the Chauchat was easier to use than heavy machine-guns (it only weighed 9 kgs, compared to the 52 kgs of a Hotchkiss), it could be moved up as close as possible to the enemy during attacks.

✦ The special Mle 1917 haversack containing 12 magazines was carried by the first ammunition supplier.

✦ A special Mle 1915 pouch containing 4 magazines was carried by the gunner and the first ammunition supplier.

✦ A semi-circular shaped magazine, an instruction manual, a speciality badge and an instruction manual for the Chauchat machine-gun.

✦ A Chauchat gunner of the 31st R.I. (Paris), which was attached to the 10th D.I. and fought at the Chemin des Dames, more precisely at the bois des Buttes. This man here is equipped with semi-circular Chauchat-specific magazine pouches as well as a prototype Adrian helmet with a Dunand visor which was issued on an experimental basis. Expecting an attack, his M2 gas mask is carried in its pouch, and not in its metal case. He is equipped with a Ruby pistol for close-quarter defence, which is not visible since it is worn at the rear. A Chauchat unit was composed of three men : a gunner and two ammunition suppliers.

LETTERS AND TRENCH NEWSPAPERS

Given the fact that they were far from their families, correspondence was an important part of the Poilus' life. Letters were the only possible link with loved ones. This explains the quantity of letters and diaries written by the soldiers. It was not rare for a soldier to send one letter a day to his family. Quite often, a postcard format photo was sent to reassure those at home.

The news sent home generally stated that all was well and was meant to comfort those who, far from the war, only heard of what was happening via a rarely objective press.

Families were also able to send parcels of food and clothing in order to help improve the daily life of their loved ones at the front. The press was also present in the trenches in the form of newspapers written by the soldiers, although these were, of course, the subject of censorship.

Censorship was widespread, even for private correspondence. Defeatists were closely watched and punished if caught.

Very few letters actually gave an honest view of the state of mind of the men in the trenches.

✦ Looked at or read by candlelight, letters and photographs of loved ones brought some humanity into the hell of the trenches. Pictures taken before the war in 1914, such as the one above, are a reminder that many are no longer here, either killed, wounded, disabled or missing in the mud of the battlefields.

✦ The 309th R.I. from Chaumont, which was attached to the 71st D.I., fought in the Vosges from 1914 to 1916, before leaving for Verdun. The Regiment was disbanded in June 1916. The photograph above was taken in 1915 in Badonviller; seen here are the seemingly uninspired writing staff of the «Echo des Marmites», the regimental newspaper.

TRENCH ART /
ART IN THE TRENCHES

Life in the trenches was not entirely taken up by fighting. During quiet periods, the soldiers tried to improve their day-to-day life, especially in the trenches.

Hunting for lice - nicknamed "totos" by the Poilus - and rats helped reduce hygiene problems. Writing letters was a way of temporarily escaping the trenches and of maintaining the bond with loved ones.

A certain inventivity came to light through various creations made by these men. Originally, carpenters, builders and others were used for building dug-outs and shelters, especially as nothing had been planned for providing shelter for the troops. Ruined villages were a source of building material and furniture that could be used to equip these shelters.

But another side of the soldiers' creativity quickly came to the fore. Continuous shelling provided plenty of scrap copper and aluminium which were sculpted and transformed into various objects and tools such as letter openers and lighters. Copper drive bands from shells and aluminium fuzes were melted and turned into items of jewellery that were taken back home and given as gifts to relatives or fiancées.

The best known of these artefacts are the engraved shell cases, but the following pictures give a somewhat broader insight into the creative abilities of these men.

✦ Despite the separation of Church and State in 1905, religion rose to prominence in reaction to the violence of the war. Pictured here are Christs attached to German bullets.

✦ Letter openers made of shell drive bands and bullets. Due to the constant shell fire, copper and brass were in abundant supply for the Poilus.

✦ Whether it be girlfriends or wives, women were absent from the trenches. This leg with a garter, most probably the work of a nostalgic Poilu who would have been thinking of a woman during the dreadful fighting at Soissons in 1917.

✦ To provide light in a dug-out, a F1 grenade, three bullets and a drop of fuel helped generate enough light to read in the dark shelters.

THE LAST SACRIFICES :
A SOLDIER OF THE 95TH R.I. IN THE TRENCHES

Following the peace treaty signed with Russia, Germany was able to concentrate all its troops on the Western Front.

France, on the other hand, could count on the support of American troops from 1917 onwards; the number of U.S. soldiers grew from 150,000 in January 1918 to two million in November. Despite lacking experience at first, these troops quickly rose up to the task.

On March 21st, the Ludendorff offensive was launched, breaking through British lines. This breakthrough was notably due to the use of assault troops on a great scale, which were a recent creation. But General Foch, by obtaining sole leadership of the ar-

mies, succeeded in counter-attacking and stopping the first offensive. Germany, which was weakened by the allied blockade, threw all its remaining strength into the battle and launched new offensives, notably on the Chemin des Dames. On May 30th, the Germans crossed the Marne river at Château-Thierry.

The situation was just as dramatic as in September 1914 : one last attack, set to be launched on July 15th, was aimed at putting the final nail in the coffin for France. This allowed the French to pull men back from the frontline.

However, the interrogation of a large number of German prisoners allowed the Allies to know the precise date of this offensive. As a consequence, the heavy German artillery barrage failed to cause any significant damage. The Allies counter-attacked on July 18th and pushed back the Germans.

The 8th of August was the black day for the German army, with the Franco-British forces retaking the initiative. From that point on, a war of movement returned after three years of stalemate in the trenches.

Despite American support, the war was still far from over. The German army, despite being weak, kept resisting and both sides continued to suffer huge losses.

It took until November 7th to see the start of the negotiations which eventually led to the signing of the armistice on the 11th in the forest of Rethondes. This brought an end to four dreadful years which saw an entire generation decimated by combat and by the new weapons that placed the violence of warfare on a whole new level.

✦ The 95th R.I. from Bourges was attached to the 16th D.I. ; they fought in the Champagne region in 1918 and took part in the Battle of the Main de Massiges hill. The soldier pictured here is armed with a Berthier 07/15 rifle and «Vengeur de 1870» type knife held on the belt. The tin for the new ARS 1918 gas mask is clearly visible here.

✦ The ARS 18 gas mask first saw large-scale issue throughout 1918 as a replacement of the M2.

MEDALS

France only had two main medals to offer when it came to rewarding its soldiers' bravery : the Légion d'honneur, created by Napoleon in 1802, and the Médaille Militaire, founded by Napoleon III in 1852.

There were two distinct orders for the Légion d'honneur : the Chevalier medal (a red ribbon, on the chest), and the Officier medal (a red «rosette», on the chest). These medals were essentially awarded to officers.

The Médaille Militaire was awarded to non-commissioned officers and to soldiers under the following conditions :
- eight years of service, or four campaigns ;
- Wounded by enemy action or whilst on active service;
- acts of bravery or sacrifice.

In order to boost morale and to reward those the most deserving, a new medal was created in 1915 : the Croix de Guerre. It is mainly thanks to LCL Driant's initiative that the law promulging the awarding of the Croix de Guerre was voted on April 8 1915.

Mentions in dispatches are the following :
- Army : a laurel-shaped bronze leaf ; a silver leaf represents five bronze leaves.
- Army Corps : a ruby red star.
- Division : a silver star
- Brigade or regiment : a bronze star.

From April 1915 onwards, the first Croix de Guerre were awarded. By the end of the conflict, more than 1.2 million men had received the medal.

It is worth noting that receiving the Médaille Militaire made one eligible for the Croix de Guerre with a palm. Finally, a wound badge was created on 27 July 1916 and consisted of a coloured bar with a five-branched star made of red enamel in the middle. The medal itself was only created in 1920.

✦ The Médaille Militaire.

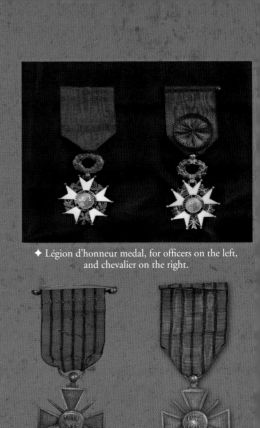

✦ Légion d'honneur medal, for officers on the left, and chevalier on the right.

✦ Two Croix de Guerre medals : the 14-15 version on the left, and the 14-16 version on the right.

✦ Two Croix de Guerre medals : the 14-17 version on the left, and the 14-18 version on the right.

✦ The Croix de Guerre, with a leaf and with a bronze star.

POST-WAR COMMEMORATIVE MEDALSCOMMEMORATIVE MEDAL.

✦ A framed display with the inter-allied medal, combatant's cross and 1914-1918 commemorative medal.

✦ Medal for the wounded.

✦ Verdun medal.

✦ Inter-allied medal.

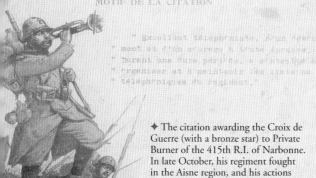

✦ The citation awarding the Croix de Guerre (with a bronze star) to Private Burner of the 415th R.I. of Narbonne. In late October, his regiment fought in the Aisne region, and his actions earned him the medal, which he received after the war.

✦ National union for war veterans medal, an organisation which remains active to this day.

HOW TO INTERPRET
A FAMILY PHOTOGRAPH

Cliché nº 1

Old photographs of relatives proudly posing in a photographer's studio during leave are common. Maybe you have wondered about that particular person in the picture - what was his unit, his rank ? When was the picture taken ?

The first, somewhat traditional photograph, shows us a soldier of the 11th R.I., the number of which is worn on the kepi as well as on the collar. The kepi and trousers are from 1915, since they are made of corduroy. At that time, helmets had not yet been issued, as was also the case with the horizon blue uniform.

On the second photograph, we can see three soldiers, all wearing an entirely blue uniform. The man on the right, wearing a garrison cap, has three

cloth stripes on his left sleeve which indicate the duration of his time at the front. One stripe was given after one year of active service at the front, and an additional one for each new six-month period; the soldier's stripes thus correspond to two and a half years of fighting. Thanks to these elements, the picture can be dated to mid-1916, given that the soldier was mobilised as early as August 1914.

The soldier in the middle, as we can deduce from his three stripes, has completed two years at the front. Stripes for wounds, which are not clearly visible here, were worn at the top of the right sleeve; in this case, the soldier has been wounded once (see photograph 3). He is also wearing, between his Croix de Guerre and Médaille Militaire, the insignia for wounded soldiers, which is only a bar as the actual medal was only created in 1920.

The soldier on the left has two canvas half-stripes at the base of his right sleeve, which indicate his rank, which could be here, according to the colour, that of senior corporal or sergeant. Once again, the number on the collar indicates the regiment.

Finally, some soldiers could wear a black band on their left sleeve as a sign of mourning.

Because of black and white photography, it is difficult to determine the background colour of the collar tabs which indicate the soldier's arm of service. Horizon blue was for infantry, red for artillery, and yellow for the light infantry regiments. Mustard was for both colonial troops and the Foreign Legion.

✦ Various collar tabs; blue or yellow for infantry, red for artillery.

Cliché nº 2

ORGANISATIONS AND SERVICES FOR RESEARCH

The first source for research is online, with the French Ministry of Defense's website: http://www.memoiredeshommes.sga.defense.gouv.fr
This website provides access to the written papers of the time, which give the circumstances and place of a fallen soldier's death by typing in a family name.

The "sépulture de guerre" website (http://www.sepulturesdeguerre.sga.defense.gouv.fr) is in the same vein. It indicates burial places and is a place of Remembrance for the Fallen. For more in-depth research there is the publication "Mort pour la France, histoire de votre ancêtre", published by Editions OREP.

The easy-to-use www.chtimiste.com website gives access to the history of each regiment, which is a great way to follow a regiment or an individual throughout the war, month by month. Other sections of the website offer more information in various domains as well as links towards other websites.

✦ The grave of Lieutenant Provost, of the 69th R.I. (Nancy and Toul), which belonged to the 11th D.I. In early 1915, the Regiment was in Belgian Flanders and took part in the Artois offensive from April to June, where Provost was killed on May 5th. He was buried by the Germans with the following epitaph: "den Heldentod für sein Vaterland", which can be translated as "the death of the hero for his country".

Cliché n° 3

BATTLEFIELD RELICS

Sometimes there is a very thin line between life and death and this is reflected in the following objects. Some seem to have been lucky, as the Lebel bullet which stopped a piece of shrapnel testifies. For others, the objects riddled with shrapnel impacts found on the battlefield are most probably the last reminder of a human life. Ninety years after the war, these relics express the violence of the the war and evoke its individual tragedies.

✦ This mess tin was found on the Chemin des Dames in 2007, after spending 91 years in the ground. It has been pulverised by shell splinters and this leads us to imagine what happened to the soldier to whom it belonged.

✦ These three objects are the testimony to the utility of helmets. The mustard-couloured helmet has been cut through by a projectile, killing its wearer. The same goes for the Adrian helmet with its cover (which was adopted in late 1915 for camouflage). The wearer of the third helmet was lucky to have it when he got hit. Without it, he would never have been able to bring this helmet home as a souvenir.

CONCLUSION

The armistice was signed on November the 11th 1918 in Rethondes, bringing an end to four years of war on a scale which had never been seen before. The "war to end all wars" caused 8.5 million deaths, 20 million wounded and crippled and the devastation of entire regions.

For many families, photographs are all that remain of a fallen relative. After the war, the bodies, which were scattered on the battlefields were regrouped in a great number of cemeteries. For those whose bodies were never found, memorials were erected in each town or village of France in memory of the war that everyone hoped would be the last.

Bodies are still being discovered to this day. If the identity tag is found with the body, identification is possible, thus allowing the fallen soldier to receive a named grave.

The survivors, the experiences of which were were so long misunderstood, have now passed away. However, they have left behind an abundance of written material as a first hand testimony of the tragedy which took away the entire youth of the 1910s.

If this booklet has aroused your curiosity regarding the military objects of this period, I can give you some advice. Start with asking around, whether it be relatives or friends. Family photographs are abundant and are a way to trace the history of an ancestor. Afterwards, car boot sales and other similar events are an almost endless source of similar documents. Even ninety years after the war, many souvenirs are to be found there, without the seller really knowing what they are. Many objects of this book were recently found at various fairs, for example.

One last important point : You may be tempted to visit the battlefields of the Great War and to bring back a few souvenirs found there. In many places, the use of metal detectors is forbidden and strictly sanctioned. More importantly, a lot of ammunition on or under ground is still lethal.

DO NOT TOUCH ANY EXPLOSIVES. Do not be fooled by the fact that they look rusty or damaged.
These weapons were meant to kill and for various reasons did not explode but they are still live. Moreover, their explosive contents have deteriorated over time, making them even more dangerous. Contact the gendarmerie and refrain from touching them. Making safe unexploded ammunition must be done professionnally since it does not have any margin for error. Every year, people die after manipulating explosives found on the battlefields.

Collecting militaria is fascinating and allows one to look at history from a different angle, through the lives of the soldiers that experienced it. Please follow the previous safety advice.

ACKNOWLEDGEMENTS

I wish to thank the collectors who helped me with this book, with their support, patience and knowledge.

First of all, thank you to my long-time friend Christian Guibelin, as without him this book would not have been possible. His collection, the fruit of more than 30 years of research, is the base of this book.
Thank you to Daniel Grobey as well, who patiently lent me his most valuable pieces.

I wish to mention Mickaël Beaulieu who gave me permission to photograph a great number of pieces of equipment, as well as everyone else who gave me access to their collection.

Finally, two shops were of great support in letting me photograph some of their best items :
- Antiquités Militaires, D.Kittler, 37 rue du Général Leclerc, 54670 Custines ; tel. : 0680169975
- Arromanches Militaria, 11 Boulevard Gilbert Longuet, 14117 Arromanches-les-bains ; tel. : 0231215104

I am always on the lookout for various documents and objects such as photographs, letters, or military equipment. You can contact me by e-mail at YT1418@aol.com

✦ As soon as the war was over, people visited the battlefields. Pictured here are walkers wearing straw boater hats at Fort-de-Vaux, a key sector of the Battle of Verdun. In 1922, four years after the war, the area was a lot quieter.